This book compliments of

www.citrixonline.com/sage

Roger Courville

The Virtual Presenter's Handbook

"Roger is the web seminar guru. Not only is he an outstanding practitioner, but he is an invaluable source of knowledge, tips, and best practice."

-Mirela Fontbernat, Director of Marketing Programs, Obiboro

1080 Group

Thank You...

To my wife Angi, and my little-but-growing-up people, Tamar, Maia, and Alden. You are my inspiration and continual reminder that there's a big difference between making a living and making a life.

Contents

Contents...

Contents...

Contents...

Delivering Like a Rockstar

Backstage

Onstage

Contents...

Section 1

Introduction

Introduction

So You're Speaking at a Web Seminar

Web seminars ("webinars") are online seminars or
presentations used to engage remote audiences with any
content that can be presented from a computer desktop.
Because presenters and audiences are connected live, web
seminars can be interactive and engaging, just like having
every person in the same room.

Web seminars are made possible by software that connects
each person via an Internet connection. Using the software
is simple, like logging into a Web site. Every person
participates aurally with audio conferencing using their
telephones or computers with headsets. Many solutions
offer video to enhance the visual connection between
teachers and learners.

Web seminars deliver many potential benefits. They reduce
travel for presenters and attendees alike. They can reach
more attendees than in-person presentations, and they may
reach attendees who otherwise could not make the in-
person presentation. They also make it possible to include
other remote presenters, who might otherwise be unable to
attend, available to reach those audiences.

Replacing 100% of face-to-face meetings shouldn't be
your goal, but the ability to dialogue (read: influence)
an audience at a distance is a unique and powerful
tool that many organizations are now adding to their
communications toolkit. And this means presenters,

speakers, marketers, trainers, executives, and a host of other roles must evolve or fall behind.

As you begin to present using web seminars, two key opportunities will emerge.

One, you can discriminate between when you really need to be face-to-face and when you don't.

Two, you can spend a lot more nights in your own bed.

Increase your reach, sleep in your own bed, travel on your own terms.

The Biggest Mistake You Can Make

You're the executive producer for a radio station, and you're meeting with a new client – the Chief Cheese who runs the company. He's decided to add a radio campaign to his go-to-market mix, and when you get to the meeting he hands you the content you used for your recent, very successful email campaign.

"Use this. It worked great."

And you say, "… uh … run that by me again?"

While admittedly dramatic, this is what happens every day in the world of live, online presentations.

A new medium demands a new approach. An in-person example would be looking at how a trainer or speaker approaches facilitating a small group discussion versus presenting to a large group. How the tables and chairs are set up, how questions are handled, etc., change based on the dynamic.

Online, you don't see your audience. You may have a choice of how the tools are configured ("presentation mode" versus "collaboration mode"). And you certainly have a new way of interacting and answering questions. The biggest mistake you can make is to do the same thing in a new place.

A new medium changes how messages are sent and received. Successful online presenters have an attitude of adaptation.

An Approach, Not a Formula

Every medium, including a presentation, has elements that you can study and repeat to improve. And knowledge comes in two forms – that which you can study and that which you simply need to experience.

What you have in your hands is a collection of thoughts gained from many years-worth and many more online presentations-worth, of experience. To call this book art would make it too subjective, but science demands a method, and there simply is no recipe for the perfect presentation, book, or web seminar.

The approach, therefore, is twofold.

The first objective is to share timeless principles with which you can approach your presentation, the technology, and your audience. This book is not written like a software manual, and there are no pictures. If it were, the minute version 2.1 of the software became version 2.2, it would be out of date.

The second objective is to communicate these principles in a practical way that you can use as a reference. You might read this book cover to cover, but I've approached it so that you can skim it, pick and choose from ideas that you can put to use immediately, and accelerate your virtual presentation mastery one idea at a time.

Textbooks and technology go out of date quickly. Principles remain.

Section 2

Getting Started

Getting Started

Where Everybody Starts

Years ago when dot-bomb money was flowing freely, the web conferencing company I worked for dropped a seven-digit sum on a usability study with one of the Big Five consulting firms. Know what they found?

New presenters barely use a "next slide" button. Maybe, MAYBE they'd use a pointer.

It's customary for presenters new to presenting online to have one of two perspectives.

The first, apprehension, is natural, and entirely explainable. Few enough folks enjoy public speaking, period, let alone doing so in a new environment.

The second, and the deadly one, is to have no fear and a bloated sense of one's own ability to 'pull off a room.' Unfortunately these folks probably aren't reading this book anyway.

Relax. Presenting online is great place to be. You can focus on your content, your voice, and your audience in a new way, and nobody will know if you left your fly is down or you dribbled coffee on your shirt twenty minutes ago.

Apprehension of something new is normal.

What Kind of Presentations Work in Live Web Seminars

Presentations fall into three general buckets – to inspire, to inform, or to influence. Some do all three.

The most common use case in web seminars is what I call edu-influence. Attract a lead, nurture it, close it, and get that person trained and using your product or service.

Fewer are the events designed to inspire – but that doesn't mean you can't do it, just that it's not currently being done much. I predict that in the future, some killer speakers will use this medium to touch emotions just like they've figured out how to do on radio or TV.

Any kind of a presentation can be a web seminar.

Webinar, Webcast, Web Seminar? Whassup with All This?

Today, it doesn't make much difference what you call it. And that's too bad, so I'd suggest reading on.

Here's a few-sentence explanation of how we got here... and what terminology might be most accurate for you.

In the beginning, web conferencing was referred to as Internet conferencing. It represented the ability to do with data (e.g., visuals, PowerPoint, desktop sharing, etc.) the same thing you could do with audio conferencing: a multi-point connection. The primary behavioral driver was the ability for real-time sharing... a visual that was as real-time as the audio connection. After all, if it's not real-time, it's pretty hard to have a conversation.

Webcasting, in its earliest form, was like broadcasting (e.g., radio or TV), albeit over the web. Like TV or radio, there was a delay... "latency," in computer lingo. It was hard to have a conversation if one side were delayed for a couple of seconds, if not many, many seconds.

Web seminars were just that – a conversation. Typically a one-to-many or few-to-many communication, the audience may mostly listen, but in many respects it's still important for everyone to be on the same page at the same time. In smaller, collaborative formats, real-time communications were important, and even when it was mostly presentation, a live Q&A session at the end still demanded the same. "Webinars" was just a contraction of "web seminars."

Over time, webcast providers added the ability to submit a question to presenters, and to confuse things more, many companies started choosing terms that they liked rather than ones that had some historical basis for the type of communication they were engaging in (including e-seminars, i-seminars, etc.).

Today, most terms are used interchangeably. We at 1080 Group are biased toward using some form of term that's descriptive of the actual meeting type (e.g., web seminar, web meeting, e-learning, etc.). But know that you will need to investigate further... and make your own decisions.

Don't get hung up on terms, but choose a technology solution that suits your presentation style.

Stories from the Front: A Tale of Two Companies

What is it that you really, really want to have happen as a result of your web seminar? I mean really want.

This point should go without saying, but it's violated so often by purveyors of crummy online presentations that it's worth tackling via a brief case study.

Consider this true story of two software companies who each obviously want to sell more product. We'll call them Gaius and Titius, and here is a comparison of how their ultimate approach was different in how they executed a web seminar program.

Product, Packaging, and Price
Gaius sells boxed software that provides sophisticated reporting and analysis. It retails for about $900.

Titius sells hosted supply-chain management software ("software as a service") and accompanying professional services. An annual engagement can run $25K to $250K.

Sales Approach
Gaius uses a small outside sales crew for major accounts, but most sales and deal qualification are done by an inside sales team. The sales cycle is ~45-60 days.

Titius uses an outside sales team. The sales cycle is six to nine months.

Demand Generation
Besides relying on the house email list of about 20,000 records, Gaius rented 100,000 email contacts from a suite of industry publishers.

Gaius has a house file of ~3500 email records. While they buy display ads in industry publications for exposure and to drive lead capture on their website, their complex sales cycle and process means they're talking to many prospects in the same large account. Most of those prospects are identified through the sales team's account management.

Primary Objective
Gaius's primary objective is the 'bounce back.' In direct mail language, this means they need the otherwise unknown lead to register for the web seminar with valid contact information so that the inside team can effectively follow up.

Titius's primary objective is thought leadership in support of the supply-chain management methodology.

Content
Gaius's content needed to create an buzzworthy event that would cut through the noise, get the attention of

press and analysts, and get cold prospects to show up. They planned a product demo around a big new product release. The opening few minutes of the web seminar was a welcome by the CEO, and this was followed by a product manager delivering features-advantages-benefits via PowerPoint and then a live product demonstration.

Titius needed to reach multiple different influencers in an account with content that spoke their language, building support and advancing the sales process. For this they called on guest presenters, primarily industry analysts, and customers who could deliver compelling case studies. Each seminar targeted a different persona in the purchasing process – economic decision makers, technical decision makers, operational influencers.

Offer & Call-to-Action
Given the primary objective of capturing a lead, Gaius opted to offer a sweepstakes-oriented offer – register for the web seminar and be entered into a drawing for a tricked-out laptop. Obviously they wanted people to attend the event, but their primary objective was accomplished simply if there was a registration with valid contact info. The nature of the giveaway ensured that prospects offered up valid contact into (versus registering anonymously with a santaclaus-@-hotmail.com-type email address). (By the way, don't go emailing Santa Claus here like hundreds of people called 867-5309 after Tommy Tutone has his 80's hit.)

Titius's need was the opposite – they needed people to attend and listen to the whole presentation. Their offer was a variety of smaller giveaways that attendees only qualified for if they stayed until the end of the event and completed the post-event survey.

Execution

Gaius scheduled their web seminar to occur in the same day, once at 7am Pacific and once at 4pm Pacific. This not only provided a choice to western hemisphere prospects, but provided business-day attendance options for EMEA and East Asia/Australia. With 5200 registered, they had ~1900 attend, meaning the quantity of questions flying in was huge. Interactivity with the audience was minimal (unfortunately!), but a few key questions were marked for answering in a Q&A session at the end of the presentation.

If you want to see how it's possible to be interactive with a thousand people in the audience, watch the recording of my presentation found here: http://bit.ly/oegtV (Note: This link was active at the time this book was published, but it may not be valid forever).

Titius, on the other hand, executed a monthly "thought leadership series." Their audiences averaged fifty in size, and they optimized interactivity between presenters and audience members by making sure presenters were prepared to answer questions throughout the presentation. This ensured attendees got their questions answered – probably as valuable to influencing them (or more) as the rest of the presentation.

The moral of this abbreviated story? A webinar is not a webinar is not a webinar - it's an event that needs to be executed according to what you really, really need or want to accomplish, by going beyond thinking about simply making an 'online presentation.'

Get specific about what you want – and plan everything else in light of that.

Section 3

Planning Your Virtual Presentation

Planning Your Virtual Presentation

How Pros Tackle Web Seminars

The key to success in any presentation is attitude. It takes a lot of work to define an outcome, understand where your audience is coming from, and plot a clear path from Point A to Point B.

Every ounce of energy you put into a presentation is an act of giving – an investment – on behalf of your audience. To begin with, you should presume your first draft isn't good enough. You should presume your charisma, your voice, your position or status, and your knowledge of the subject isn't enough. Write, edit, practice, refine, and practice again.

Remember, even Tiger Woods has a coach.

Assume your presentation can improve. It can't hurt, and it'll force you to grow.

Three Pillars of Great Online Presentations

You're making a presentation for a reason. You have a goal in mind. You must remember this: You need to adapt to a "What's next?" and, "That's nice, but how do I remember all this?" mindset.

How, you ask? The Three Pillars: purpose, movement, interactivity.

Great live, online presentations are delivered with purpose, movement, and interactivity.

WIIFM?

The audience doesn't care about you. Unless you're an acknowledged guru or a head of state, let me make sure I've said that clearly:

The audience doesn't care about you.

What they care about is, *"What's in it for me?"*

Use this knowledge to clarify your purpose before you even think about designing slide #1.

The first pillar, Purpose, answers "What's in it for me?"

Oh, My Wandering Eyes

Increasingly our culture is playing with Crackberries while they're surfing television channels. And unlike an in-person audience, your online audience can change the channel... quickly. If you keep it interesting, they'll come back. Later in the book we'll cover how to make and keep it interesting. If you don't keep it interesting, well…

The second pillar, Movement, challenges attendees not to wander away for too long.

Movies Are for Watching

Human short-term memory holds a limited amount of stuff. It's like computer RAM… if the content doesn't get saved to a hard drive, it's gone.

Your goal is to influence your audience's knowledge or skills, and their goal is related; their *"What's in it for me?"* is an expectation. Your job is to help them with the question, *"So how are you going to help me remember this?"*

Without driveling on about learning theory, trust me on one thing: Adults learn more when actively engaged than when passively watching.

The third pillar, Interactivity, is critical to memory and influence. Converse or die.

Point B

The goal of this book is your goal: a great presentation. The good news is that the elements of a great presentation apply online as well as off.

First, begin with a clear 'Point B." That is, be very clear on your desired audience outcome. What should they think, feel or do as a result of your presentation?

Second, define a clear "Point A." This would be where your audience is today on the subject at hand. It represents your understanding of their wants, needs, and aspirations.

Getting your audience from Point A to Point B is best when the route is shortest... a straight line. It involves defining a clear problem or pain, their current (or perceived) situation, and it requires you to begin by stating what you're going to tell them about how you're going to help them, stating how you're going to get them to the solution, and reiterating your points in a conclusion and call to action.

As Zig Ziglar once put it, "If you aim at nothing, you're sure to hit it."

The key elements of any presentation apply: You need to get them to Point A to Point B.

Starting Your Story

Presentation planning should begin with planning a good story. The slide and graphics that support the telling of that story come second.

Brainstorm various ideas, quotes, facts, graphics and other visual reminders onto sticky notes or index cards. There are at least two benefits to this.

One, you'll more easily see the big picture, helping you arrange a point-by-point connection between Point A and Point B.

Two, unless you're a wizard with computer-based graphics and shapes, brainstorming will likely make it much easier to sketch out visualizations that communicate key points, meaning less time spent to figure out what to do when you open PowerPoint.

Start outside PowerPoint. Start on paper.

If You Begin in PowerPoint...

Maybe there isn't time, maybe it's not your style. But if you must start creating your presentation inside PowerPoint, do so in "slide sorter" view. This will give you a similar big-picture view to laying out your sticky notes or index cards.

If you start inside PowerPoint, use the with a "slide sorter" view like sticky notes.

Planning a Great Kickoff

I once spent time on the road for one of the largest in-person seminar companies in the world, and learned a valuable lesson that applies in the virtual world.

My coach there encouraged me to consider what was absolutely necessary to my message, and lead with that, delaying sharing other information until later in my presentation. His point – a great one – was that you should lead only with the information that answers the audience's unspoken questions:

"What am I going to get out of this?"
"What is your credibility (why should I listen to you)?"

In that environment we had no moderator... we were completely on our own.

In the online world, most of the time you'll have someone who can introduce you, even if that's just the operator from the telephone company.

Remember the audience came for a meal. The sooner you can deliver an appetizer, the sooner you'll have them engaged. Other information that doesn't serve the purpose of getting them hooked can be shared later.

Dispense with long openings. Get them hooked.

Finishing As Well As You Began

Similarly, you lose your opportunity to leave the audience on a high note if your presentation ends with hesitation, a lack of definition, or a lingering Q&A session that peters out with you waiting to see if one last timid soul will speak out.

A great ending, by contrast, will create momentum. The exact content will depend on the purpose of your presentation. This could be a clear call to action, description of next steps, or a motivational high note that leaves them with a positive emotion. But whatever it is, you want to be purposeful in thinking through.

Ask yourself, "How am I going to close in order to give my audience a little bounce in their step?"

Avoid the trailing, indefinite ending.

Designing a User Experience

What Determines How You'll Interact

Remember, Point B is where you want your audience to end up. You begin with a call to action, something you want them to apply, something you want them to feel.

There is no magic bullet for the "right" way to engage a virtual audience. You might be selling or needing to advance the sale to consensus on terms. You might be training and needing the team to adequately engage trainees with a role-playing exercise to test their interviewing skills. You might be delivering a product marketing demo that achieves a goal of signups for trial accounts. Whatever it is, the right exercise is determined by how you need people to engage.

Where you want to take the audience determines how you'll interact.

The Best Interactivity Begins Here

If you're making a virtual presentation, it's likely you've previouvsly made one in person. But even if you haven't, this idea still applies.

When we speak to a group of people, there are natural ways we interact (or should learn to do). From an opener that asks, "Give me a show of hands from everybody who traveled over a hundred miles to get here today," to responding to a 'hand up' in the audience, unless you're a keynote speaker who is paid to be the entertainment, the odds are that there is some measure of interactivity in the way you engage an audience.

When the online presentation environment is unnatural to a presenter, it's common for the presenter to do unnatural things. To grow past this quickly, begin with doing what you'd do in person. This will give you a jumpstart on imagining how you'll accomplish your goal virtually and which tools you'll need to do so.

Imagine how you would interact with an in-person audience.

When NOT to Plan Interactivity

Is there ever a time not to use the interactivity tools provided?

To be sure, in most cases you should push yourself to use more and more interactivity as your audience has less distance to travel to Distraction Avenue. I'm not saying it won't feel artificial sometimes to ask a question, but your goal for that question, poll, or 'hand up' may well be to demonstrate that you *will* be interacting with the audience. This is a powerful message if you need them to engage – and you probably do if your goal is to educate and influence.

But the worst thing you can do is lose one precious moment working on something that doesn't support your presentation goals. Creating a moment of interactivity with no purpose is a waste of the audience's time… and a waste of yours.

Don't use interactivity without a reason.

When Normal Isn't Natural

Back to the theme of 'this is a new medium' for a moment. Remember two things: We optimize engagement and influence when we interact, and we need to increase how frequently we do it for an online audience.

If you're normal, this means you'll need to be thoughtful and purposeful about interacting with your online audience. Don't expect it to be natural. You won't hear the chuckles that communicate to you that your joke just landed, and you can't count on your charisma to carry the day. You have to demonstrate that if they type something into the chat or Q&A box, you're listening.

Plan interactivity into the presentation.

Section 4

What to Know About Virtual Presentation Technology: Choosing the Right Tools

What to Know About Virtual Presentation Technology: Choosing the Right Tools

Getting Started

A VFAQ (very frequently asked question) is, "How do I keep my audience from multi-tasking?" And the first thing I want to say is, "Don't be boring."

A kinder, gentler response is this. We live in an era of Blackberries, iPhones, laptops with mobile access and Twitter users tweeting in the middle of a presentation. The real answer is you have to deal with your audience multi-tasking whether you're in-person or virtual.

Consider this: Pilots are taught to fly both by sight and by instruments only, when they can't see anything. They're two separate skill sets.

Choosing the right tools begins with realizing they're your lifeline to connecting to the audience you can't see. A complete set of presentation skills, when you're going to present online, requires you to adapt to the medium.

And much like a pilot, you're going to have to learn to fly by instruments for success.

Tools are your steering wheel, compass, and altimeter.

One Size Doesn't Fit All

You've been to keynote presentations, hands-on workshops, collaborative strategy sessions, and new-hire trainings. And for the sake of brevity, I'm assuming you've delivered some of them.

As a speaker at an in-person event, the way you work the room depends on your audience, your objective, how many attendees are in front of you… even how the room is configured. And ideally you've been part of choosing how the tables and chairs are arranged.

Web and audio conferencing tools often allow you to choose different "seating arrangements," too.

Like the in-person session, you'll be more collaborative and flexible with a smaller audience. You can ask and answer more questions or even let others contribute (such as drawing on a whiteboard). With a larger audience you'll need more structure.

As you grow in your virtual presentation skills, you will discover that different providers offer different configurations of tools that facilitate interaction. Some are better suited to large audiences, some for smaller audiences. Some providers give you a choice of configurations (often between "meeting" products and "webinar" products).

A great place to start is by thinking through how you would present and interact if the audience was in the same room with you. Would you ask for a show of hands? Would meeting members take turns at a whiteboard? Would there be a panel of speakers, or a moderator, or...? Would you use a microphone in the middle of the room, allowing a limited number of audience members to ask questions, or when many hands go up, respond only to a portion of them?

After you've thought through these questions, choose the best configuration of tools for your virtual meeting. Some solutions allow you to pick and choose what you turn on and off. Others offer a "meeting" option versus a "seminar" option.

And it's worth noting... if you can't choose the right tools for the job, do you have the right solution?

Optimize your impact. Choose the right virtual seating arrangement.

Audio: Listening In

Think about a seminar you've attended with hundreds of people in the audience. The presenter has a certain amount of content to get through in a specified period of time.

Now put yourself in the presenter's shoes. You've planned how to interact with your audience, and ideally you've got a sense of how much time you will spend doing it.

If you need to retain maximum control over your presentation, you need to be able to pick and choose which questions you respond to. Ideally you can choose questions that best support your point, best provide value to the broadest part of your audience, best set you up to be the rockstar.

The only way you can do that is to manage questions via text. This means that your best solution for letting the audience listen is having them on "listen only" mode, whether they're on the telephone or listening over their computers.

Put the audience on "listen only" for optimum control.

One-Way, or Interactive?

Full, two-way audio connections are sometimes valuable. They put every member of the audience in a co-equal place with the presenter. This might be ideal for a small meeting or training session when everyone is engaged and paying attention to what's going on.

In most e-seminar settings, however, open audio lines are fraught with trouble.

First, many phone systems will play hold music if an attendee puts a conference line on hold to take another call. And the one thing you can't do is ask the person not to do it... they can't hear you.

Second, attendees may be tempted to put you on speakerphone, opening up the probability that you'll hear typing, coughing, dog barking, or even the building air conditioner coming on in the background.

Finally, anybody can ask anything. This might be okay in many meeting settings, but as often as not in a presentation, you need to control messaging and deal with some questions offline.

For example, in nearly every presentation I make for a conferencing vendor, someone asks about price or how this vendor's service compares to the competition. The last thing we want to be addressing in a public environment is some corner case, some off-the-deep-end subject, or a value question that we don't have an adequate opportunity to explore and answer correctly.

Open audio lines presents open risk for background noise... or worse.

To VoIP, or Not to VoIP...

The use of VoIP (Voice over Internet Protocol) is on the rise. The technology has been around for a long time, but there are many reasons it has only recently emerged in mainstream usage.

The up side of using computer-based conferencing is price. It's cheap, often available for a fixed fee, and often now built into web conferencing platforms and their pricing packages. This is especially good news for large audiences, and even better for international participants with high calling rates.

But there are some downsides, too. Early on, VoIP wasn't terribly friendly with firewall technologies, and users external to an organization often experienced problems. It also it makes the local computer and its local internet service – the least reliable part of the web conferencing experience – a single point of failure. If the computer locks up, for example, both the audio and video components of the conference are halted.

Today the technology is better than ever. But remember these things:

Most attendees will listen over their computers, but won't have a headset installed. This means, like the "listen only" audio model, that you're going to want to be facile with text-based Q&A. Also, if your audience is of decent size, the odds are still good that someone will note, "I can't hear the audio." It doesn't make any difference if this is a user-error or not (it often is – they don't have their speakers turned on or their corporate network settings block certain kinds of traffic) – it will still be a distraction.

Still, the cost savings is alluring. Know your audience, know your goals, know your tolerance for perfection.

VoIP is better than ever, but know your risks and tradeoffs.

Integrate, Integrate, Integrate

Some conferencing providers have some form of audio integrated into their service – teleconferencing, VoIP, or both. A key benefit to this is the time it takes to set up a meeting.

Scheduling a meeting may seem like a simple task, but consider what happens as you increase your frequency of usage. If web and audio are separate services, you'll schedule the web conference, schedule the audio conference, and then have to make sure attendees get the right phone number. *Then* you'll have separate call details necessary for presenters – another scheduling activity. Worse, the minute somebody has to ask again for the details (not if, but when!), you go searching again.

Integrated audio options mean you'll be scheduling one meeting. Further, the confirmation emails and reminder emails will have the correct audio information (no chance of copy/pasting the wrong thing).

Beyond this, some services allow you to schedule your web and audio conferencing through your calendar. Given that you would otherwise have to find or remember the URL of the web site you use to schedule your meeting/ presentation, navigate there, login, do your scheduling, and *then* put it on your calendar... this can be a significant time saver.

All told, when you do this frequently or repeatedly, you'll see that the number of clicks it takes to execute a task can be reduced by fifty to seventy percent when you use an integrated audio solution. And who needs to add more tasks to their day?

Integrated audio saves setup time for frequent meetings.

Somebody's Gotta Pay

Of increasing popularity, especially with the aforementioned integrated audio options, is audio conferencing that requires each attendee to dial a toll-based number. There are three reasons this isn't always a bad thing.

One, most people's domestic long distance costs are negligible. In many locales a home or cell phone has unlimited long distance calling.

Two, in a corporate environment, those costs are often even lower, and most employees have zero need to track costs. They don't think twice about dialing a long distance call.

Three, the barriers to international calling are coming down. Toll-free calls for international participants are cumbersome and generally expensive, but dialing directly is easy. And inexpensive if they're using Skype or a similar service.

Know your audience, and offer a toll-free audio conferencing option if it really would be a barrier to entry for them. Odds are it's not.

Toll-free audio is a nice audience benefit, but make sure the benefits outweigh the additional cost.

Screen Sharing

There is nothing quite as defining and powerful in web conferencing as the ability to show anything on your desktop. From collaborating on a document or brainstorming on a whiteboard, to making a presentation or demonstrating a software program to a thousand people, screen sharing makes it possible to have a flexible, powerful visual element accompanying an audio dialogue.

A few quick screen sharing tips that will save you some heartache:

One, close other applications, especially email and instant messaging. More than one embarrassing moment has occurred when a message pops up while the presenter is sharing a screen.

Two, check your options. Many web conferencing vendors allow you to choose whether you share your whole desktop or only a specific application (such as PowerPoint or Excel, the software or web browser you intend to demonstrate, etc). This may allow you to go back and forth between what you're showing the audience and something else you want or need to refer to.

Three, remember there might be times when you don't want to screen share. Some services integrate PowerPoint in such a way (such as uploading) that it performs better than when you share it from your screen. Often these services integrate polls or other media in ways that make your presentation flow much more smoothly.

Screen sharing is powerful. Know your options and risks.

Blooper Story

We had a client at Microsoft who was having a smallish seminar, and while he wanted all lines muted while he was presenting, he wanted open audio lines for the Q&A session. He's paying the bill, so we reluctantly agreed.

In the middle of his Q&A session all participants the audio line was suddenly flooded with the sound of a woman in the throes of passion. As you might expect, all voices stopped, only emphasizing the NSFW (not suitable for work) noises.

While we'll never know if one web seminar attendee was actually getting lucky or was simply multi-tasking in his browser with his computer speakers on, the presenter (to his credit) recovered quickly quipping,

"Well, at least someone's enjoying themselves here."

Keyboard and Mouse Control

I recommend presenting with a partner whenever possible. They might be co-presenting, answering questions in the background, or acting as a moderator and serving up questions and comments.

That said, be aware that different services handle multiple presenters in different ways. Some give every presenter co-equal access to controls (know who's on first base!), while others provide different levels of access, or require presenters to pass control back and forth.

The biggest hiccups aren't typically technological, they're logistical. And logistics are easy to manage with communicaton... and a bit of rehearsal.

Questions to ask yourself: How will the call be kicked off? How is the person delivering the welcome going to introduce and pass control to the first presenter? How are questions going to be handled?

Know who has the football.

Attention Detectors

Some solutions provide services that allow you to keep an eye on your audience with an 'attentiveness meter' or similar tool. This typically works simply by detecting the active window on an attendee's computer.

Some conferencing providers in the e-learning space allow you to see this data on an individual-by-individual basis. This would be useful for smaller, collaborative meetings, without too many people to keep track of.

Other vendors simply aggregate this data and let you know what percentage of the audience is actively viewing at any given moment. For larger audiences this is more than adequate.

Either way, it's a useful tool for monitoring your audience. If you see attentiveness begin to decline (just like you might notice a few surreptitious yawns when you're in person), you can adjust, change the energy, ask a question or a poll, or take a break.

One note: Don't expect 100% of your audience to be paying attention (and don't take it personally). And if you want to watch the number jump, just mention that you have an attentiveness meter and are keeping an eye on it.

Keep an eye on your audience.

Polls

Polls are tools built into many web conferencing services. Usually they offer an opportunity to ask a multiple-choice question, and many offer you choices about when to share the results with the audience.

Some services also offer the ability to ask an open-ended question. This can be handy if you'd like to solicit feedback or comments that aren't easily put into a multiple-choice format.

Be aware of how the poll appears to your audience. Some appear in place of whatever you are presenting. That means that your presentation flow might include planning to share poll results between slides four and five, for example. Other polls may appear to the side of the presentation content.

Some services make it easier than others to create a poll on the fly. Depending on the nature of your presentation, creating a poll on the fly might be a valuable way to get instant, quantifiable feedback from your audience.

Finally, many services capture polling information by individual for the post-event report. Is it important to you know which people voted "yes" when you asked a particular question? Simply having a poll available doesn't necessarily mean you'll get what you need.

Polling tools are varied and flexible. Know your options.

Why Polls Are Your Friend

Polls are excellent, multi-purpose tools. Consider a few of the many things you can do:

Get people engaged right away.
When speaking, sometimes an opening question isn't so much about the answer someone gives as much as a way to get them engaged and demonstrate to the audience

that you're going to interact. Polls make great opening questions.

Relate to content on a slide.
This is easier if the poll appears at the side of the screen instead of inline, but the principle is the same.

Imagine, theoretically, that you ask the audience to draw a house. Then you put up four different pictures of houses and ask the audience to choose, A, B, C, or D, which one their drawing most closely resembles. You might even give them an E, soliciting freeform text entry that lets them share a description of what they drew (hint: you can use Q&A or chat function for this, too).

Learn how to frame your presentation.
Ask an early question, via poll, to assess the audience's experience, desires, or expectations.

Use polls to learn from your audience, adjust on the fly and improve your dialogue.

Chat

Chat is like instant messaging, and it generally comes in one of a few flavors.

Everybody can chat with everybody.
Everyone can chat with each other. This might be handy for a smaller, collaborative meeting or presentation. But the last thing you want in the middle of a presentation is some disgruntled heckler chatting with everyone saying,

"Competitor X is WAAAAY cheaper," or something equally harmful.

Participants can only chat with presenters.
There are several variations of this. In some solutions, it's a Q&A function. In others it might be a separate function so participants can only chat with presenters, and perhaps only if the presenter initiates the chat first.

Presenters chat with presenters.
Even when audience chat is turned off, it's handy for presenters to be able to chat with each other. In the event of problems, giving a long-winded co-presenter a time check, or having a behind-the-scenes question manager serving up a question to the speaker, the chat option can be very helpful.

Not all event communication is presenter-to-audience. Use chat to improve everybody's experience.

Be Careful!

A couple ideas for you when using chat...

As with email, double check who you're sending your comment to before pushing the 'send' button. The last thing you want is to send the wrong thing to the wrong person.

And make sure you know what the audience will see. It's not common these days, but there was a time when chat appeared as a pop-up for some vendors. If this is the case for you, it's likely that it will simply appear as a black box to the audience. But in the really ancient days (a few years ago) that wasn't the case. See 'Blooper Story' below.

Be communication smart. Double check before pushing the "submit" button.

Blooper Story

I was once asked by an account manager to join her on a call with a $700K-per-year client. The objective was to demonstrate an advanced registration system on which I was expert "It's a done deal," she said, "and this is the final meeting to answer any remaining questions."

After asking the client a few exploratory questions, I began screen sharing to demonstrate the system. Part of the way through the demonstration a woman in the audience started grilling me fiercely. And I don't mean she was just asking hard questions, she was hostile.

To be sure, I don't get flustered easily, especially when I'm expert at something (like I was at the time with online registration systems). And I didn't get flustered this time. Nonetheless, the account manager decided to use web conferencing tool's chat function to send me a message...

It might have been funny, seeing the account manager get flustered and embarrassed in front

of me, calling her client a b**** and all, except that
(you guessed it), the chat came up while I was
sharing my screen with God and country.

Needless to say, while we didn't lose the entire
account, we didn't close that particular deal.

Hand Up

A 'hand up' feature is an indicator for audience members
to use to give presenters a notification – commonly
because they want to ask a question. Services with this
feature allow the presenters see who has their hand up
(based on how the person logged in, so someone logging
in as Santa Claus is, well, you decide).

Some services with integrated audio features allow
presenters to respond by changing the attendee from
listen-only audio to an open audio line (and back). If
you need to control the audio environment but want to
manage Q&A yourself (versus using an operator-assisted
audio conferencing solution), this can be a valuable
benefit.

Use a hand-up feature to identify and call on attendees.

Text Q&A

Text-based Q&A is your friend. If you learn no other
tools, become facile with this one.

Text Q&A is the key to engaging an audience interactively while maintaining order and momentum. Seeing questions come in while you present is like watching hands go up in an audience, except better... you know what they're asking and can decide whether or not to answer.

In terms of the tool itself, most vendors' Q&A can be captured. Get to know what you've got – some are available in a post-event report, while others may not capture the goods this way (you can always highlight/copy/paste before closing out of the event).

And often the Q&A view given to the presenters can be "undocked," "floated," or otherwise separated from other tools. This usually means you can expand the window, giving you a large view to keep an eye on – especially handy because you're now going to be an interactive presenter and have lots of questions, and because you don't want to spend time scrolling through piles of them.

Get to know your text-based Q&A options.

Make It a Habit

If interactively engaging your audience isn't your paradigm, you've probably already put this book in the round file and aren't reading this. For the rest of you, I'm going to exhort you to get that Q&A pane undocked and open in front of you.

It's simple: If it's open, you can glance at it in a fraction of a second... while audience members are answering a poll, while a moderator or co-presenter is speaking, or when you pause on purpose to do so.

Text Q&A isn't something to navigate to occasionally. Have it open in front of you.

Six Ways Text-Based Q&A Is Superior for Presenters

• You can them ignore respondents for a while without someone *feeling* ignored... or passing out from holding their arm up too long.

• Have you ever heard the phrase "parking lot?" When a question comes in that you'd really rather answer later one-on-one instead of in front of the group, text Q&A is a very good thing.

• You can pick and choose the questions you want to want to answer.

• You can better manage your time.

• You can use planted questions more easily.

• You can tackle them as a group. For a big audience, you can enlist additional people to join the presentation team to answer questions. Let the event producer, moderator, or sales team tackle those FAQs that would otherwise take up your time.

Annotation Tool

Annotation tools are your instruments for pointing, highlighting, drawing, and writing on your screen. Since your audience can't see you, they improve your ability to communicate visually in three ways:

One, they let you direct attention.

Two, they add visual interest of the presentation. Something is moving, and your audience will naturally look at what is moving.

Three, when combined with a virtual whiteboard, presenters have a solid replacement for a flipchart.

To get started with annotation tools, consider finding one tool that suits you and your presentation, and get comfortable with it. Don't sweat learning them all... over time you'll naturally grow from grabbing the one you're comfortable with to grabbing one right next to it.

Start with one annotation tool. The rest will come.

Handouts

Not all web seminar solutions make it possible to share a handout (and there may be other ways to distribute a handout, such as upon registration or in a follow-up "thank you for attending" email).

If you have the ability to use handouts virtually, ask yourself the same question you would ask if you were presenting face-to-face: "What's the purpose of the handout?"

Some handouts simply summarize the presentation. Distributing these in advance of the presentation risks someone glancing ahead and then tuning out.

Other handouts are designed to give attendees a place to take notes, thus reinforcing your content as you deliver it.

Personally, I use post-event handouts to accomplish three things:

One, I summarize just the top-level presentation points. Since I distribute handouts with a link to the recording, I don't try to write out all the presentation points. The summary will be a reminder for those paying attention, and if someone wants all the goodies, they can watch the recording.

Two, I include additional links to resources that I couldn't or shouldn't cover in the presentation. This adds value, and creates "stickiness" for point number three...

Three, I always include my contact information at the end of the handout. It's tasteful, but it makes it easy for someone who might otherwise have forgotten "who made that presentation" to find me, my blog, my company, my book, etc.

One final note: GREAT presentation slides make AWFUL handouts. If someone can read all your slides, your slides probably suck.

Great handouts take the pressure off your slides to serve as documents and add additional value.

Video

I am often asked about the use of video. Full-motion video is a tool like any other. The question I always ask inquirers is, "What are you going to do with video that you can't otherwise do without it?"

There are completely legit reasons for using video. I once worked with an aftermarket car parts manufacturer who wanted to have a cameraman walk around a car – at the prompt of an audience question – to show the car part in question. Completely valid. And video is a great addition to a smaller, collaborative meeting.

More often the use of video is simply a crutch for the rest of the presentation not moving. You can fix that by fixing your presentation.

Another reason people ask for video is for the sake of personalization. While I understand, I don't think the "cost" (technological, not economic) is worth the hassle. Adding a picture of yourself at the beginning and end of the presentation is often sufficient, and if you wanted you could add more in the middle.

Is video the only way to show what you need to show?

Types of Video – A Primer

The primary reason I'm not a fan of video (and cover it lightly in this book) is this: In its current forms it doesn't well serve the average presenter.

Your audience has a pretty high expectation for video performance. This is because video works well over the web... when it's on demand. Whether cruising YouTube or ABC News, or catching up on the first season of Friday Night Lights, if you've got a broadband connection, it works pretty well.

But live, multi-point video isn't so easy.

Consider the three general forms of video on the market today, shared here in pretty simple terms.

The best quality experience is delivered by dedicated video conferencing systems (for the knowledgeable among you I'm lumping telepresence into this bucket). Cameras are installed at two or more endpoints, and share their video with those same endpoints. The quality of that audio/visual experience is good because of how they're connected. They may or may not conveniently allow presenters to share a presentation or other data content.

There are two downsides for average joe orgs. Dedicated systems range from moderately priced (S5-15K) to seriously expensive (S200K+). Worse, you still have to go somewhere to use them – it's not available at the desktop. That leaves out teleworkers, travelers, etc., and it leaves out ad hoc communications.

The next two forms, peer-to-peer and streaming video, have some serious tradeoffs. The good news is that they are available at the desktop. The bad news is that they rely on the stability and throughput speed of your desktop computer and local web connection – and those the weakest links in the chain.

Streaming video is the oldest delivery mechanism, and commonly uses Windows Media Player or Real Media. Here's how it works.

Nobody wants to watch video or listen to music that is choppy. To accommodate this, streaming media players "buffer" the video. In other words, the internet delivers bits of information (called "packets") to your computer in a choppy way. It's like a stream running down hill that flows into a pool, fills, then runs out the other side. Even when the input is uneven, the output is smooth.

The problem with streaming video is delay ("latency"). By definition, the buffering time causes some delay, and the availability of bandwidth fluctuates, causing more delay. This is okay for the video (and audio, which come through the same stream), but it doesn't work well (or at all) for real-time dialogue. Text questions submitted by the audience are delayed by that same factor because the audience is responding after they see the delayed video. And a live phone connection for questions would require a clunky workaround.

Peer-to-peer video solves this by making a direct connection from the video source to the attendee's desktop. To make this work, though, the video is typically small and highly compressed, and it's still not uncommon to experience a little choppiness or hesitation. Peer-to-peer works much better for real time communication, but the downside is that it doesn't scale to larger audiences.

Peer-to-peer video is can be used for smaller, collaborative sessions when you want multi-point video – everybody can see everybody. As you can imagine, you don't have to have very many participants for this to become a useless idea for a presenter.

Finally, remember that most problems aren't technological – vendors sell good products. Most problems are logistical (often on the side of the attendee). At least one benefit you gain when you lower the barrier to participation is that you increase the odds of a successful experience for your attendees.

Ask yourself, what do you really need video for?

Video is a tool. Use it only when it's the right tool for the job.

Webcam

When a presenter stands at a podium or lectern, where do they look? Mostly at the audience... and they may occasionally glance at their slides or notes.

When at a computer, however, the tendency is to look at your slides.

But when you do that, what is someone watching via webcam seeing?

Your forehead.

The surest way to lose an authentic connection with your audience (any audience, really) is to not make eye contact. Simply reading what's on a slide only adds insult to injury.

Look at the webcam, not at the presentation. Glance at your notes no more or less than when in person.

How Roger Presents

I cover up most of the presentation. 'Tis true, and here's why.

One, I generally use highly visual slides. I don't need to read them.

Two, I have a printed copy of my slides, using PowerPoint's "notes" view, so my notes are on the printed copy.

Three, I don't use annotation tools (except when a presentation specifically calls for them). The reason is twofold – First, I have slides that I flip through at a rapid pace. Second, I don't need to point to something on the slide, because my slides are simple, uncluttered, and communicate one point per slide.

Four, I stand up to present (or go back and forth between standing up and sitting down). It boosts my energy, and you hear it in my voice.

Five, if possible, I undock two tools. The first is the Q&A screen which I make as tall as my screen will allow, at a width of about a third of my screen. This usually covers up the left third of the presentation. The second is the presenter chat box. I don't chat except in emergencies, but I have it available. I don't want to go looking for it and have to open it in order to see it. This too covers up part of the presentation.

So with my presentation covered up with tools, what gives? Let me ask you the same question. If you're not reading your slides, and assuming you've rehearsed and you know where your deck is going, what do you need to look at?

The reality is that all you need at this point is a 'next slide' button, whether that's clicking on the slide itself, using the down arrow, or using a control on the presenter console.

Section 5

Adapting Slides to the Virtual Stage

Adapting Slides to the Virtual Stage

Text and Language

Remember that our goal is to influence and impact even those who are half asleep or two threads into a Blackberry email thread. To that end, one tactic for making it as easy as possible to communicate your point is to put the key point or concept in the title of the slide.

Other benefits to you: It'll help you keep content on the slide focused on the subject you present in the title, and when you lay out your slides in 'slide sorter' view it'll be easy to read from point to point to make sure the big picture of your presentation logically follows from idea to idea.

Put the key point in the slide title.

Don't Be Boring

When you put the key point in the title of the slide, use active verbs whenever possible to make your point with greater power. Consider the following two titles:

- •Q3 results are down year-over-year

- •Q3 YOY decrease demands attention

Use active verbs.

Outlined Text (AKA Bullet Points)

Many presenters quip that bullets are for guns, and true enough, more than a few folks have died in their sleep from an onslaught of outline bullets. But sometimes they're necessary, and a genuine few of you may not have the time or skills to get past them (okay, I don't really believe you don't have the skills, and if you don't have time to do it right, when will you find time to do it over... but I digress).

A bullet point is simply using text in an outline format. The goal of bullet points, if you're going to use them, is to make sure your content is quickly readable. If you're going to use words, turn sentences into fragments that distill the essence of what you need to say.

Sentence fragments are okay. It's an outline.

Bad Example – Sales Order Process

English majors would remind us that you don't put a period at the end of the text in a bullet point.

Eliminate periods after bullet point.

New Sales Order Process

- Customer faxes purchase order to central sales fax number or emails it to the account rep.
  - Must be signed
  - Must have all pages included or you won't get commission
- Account rep updates the online sales CRM system with all appropriate detail and prints an internal sales order.
- Account rep delivers copy of internal order and signed purchase order to Trina in order management.
- Account rep sends thank you email from online sales CRM system to customer.

Less Than Less Is More

You might have heard of a rule to guide the creation of slides, something like the '5 X 5' rule – no more than five bullet points with no more than five words each.

Scrap it.

The goal of such an idea is laudable. It forces a bit of brevity, and the editing process usually crisps up the message a bit. But your core problems still remain because people:

• Read faster than you speak
• Glaze over when presented with text
• Multitask and won't be working hard to get your message

And our goal is influence, which only happens when we impart knowledge and change behavior.

The answer is to use even less. Maybe a key word or three. Or better yet, turn the content into something visual.

Forget "5X5." Cut it down. Then use even less.

Poor Example, But Better Than Bad Example

New Sales Order Process

- Customer faxes signed, complete purchase order
- Update CRM system
- Deliver internal order and purchase order to order management
- Send system-generated thank you email

This book isn't a treatise on grammar, but it does have the goal of making you a better presenter. When using bullet points, don't forget to pay attention to your grammar. Your content will be easier for your audience to grasp quickly, and you won't have the English grads snickering.

Consider the following propositions in the following set of instructions... which one doesn't fit?

- Receive the faxed contract
- Update the sales database
- Internal routing form is filled out in duplicate
- File the hard copy within 24 hours

If you imagine each instruction preceded by "you," it's easy to see that the third bullet point doesn't read as cleanly as it could ("Complete the internal routing form in duplicate" would be better).

Remember parallel sentence structure and verb agreement.

Visualize It

Continuing with the previous example, which words provide instruction? It's the verbs – "receive," "update," "complete," "file."

So how could you turn this into a visual? In this case, the relationship is linear... you complete one action before the next. At least one way to represent this relationship visually is with arrows:

Receive -> Update -> Complete -> File

Before you've even added a single shape or color, you've already created a visual representation that much more quickly communicates a process. And you don't have to be an expert designer to use the 'auto shapes' function in PowerPoint to create boxes or arrows around these words, adding a whole new dimension and level of impact to your communication.

Turn words into visuals whenever possible.

Less Poor Example – Sales Order Process

New Sales Order Process

* ~~Customer faxes signed, complete purchase order~~
* Receive purchase order from customer
* Update CRM system
* Deliver internal order and purchase order to order management
* Send system-generated thank you email

More on Turning Words into Visuals

Legendary presentation coach Jerry Weisman (*Presenting to Win*, and *The Power Presenter*) teaches a concept that he calls "graphic synchronization." He describes it as a union of design (what you show) and what you say. When presenting via web conferencing the audience isn't seeing your literal body language, so this is more important than ever. The visuals you're using in your presentation on replaces your body language.

You don't have to be an artist or designer to create visual slides, and a key benefit is that it will reduce your temptation to read what's on the slide. What you will need to invest – on behalf of your audience – is your time.

Whenever possible, create slides that are simple and visual.

Best Example – Sales Order Process

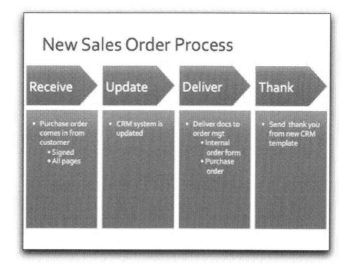

Auto-Mate

If finding "just the right graphic" is a time-consuming proposition (it is), one way to create visual slides that takes a lot less time is using auto-shapes. Built into PowerPoint, Keynote, et al, are simple-to-create squares, arrows, circles, etc. that can be used to add dimension to your concepts.

There isn't always a relationship to be represented, but look for one. Is there motion, sequence, parent-child or other relationship being represented that will suggest what shapes to use and where to place them? Get clear on the key concept of the slide and you'll have a better idea what to create. Try to communicate too much on one slide and it'll be confusing at best, a complete mess at worst.

Use auto-shapes to turn words into visuals.

Making the Best of Your Templates

Presentation software is based on the idea of templates. Graphic elements such as colors and fonts are chosen thematically for a template. If you're not a designer (and you're not starting from scratch), using the color palette in a template will bring a visual cohesiveness to your presentation without you having to work at it or second-guess yourself. And the good news is that your organization probably already has a template provided by marketing that will ensure your auto-shape choices present the organization's look and feel.

Leverage the colors in the color palette.

Don't Date Yourself

A quick note about the tools built into your presentation software: While shapes are universal and eternally accepted as ways to represent ideas, tools like clip art that come with your software should be avoided.

The reason is this: Anything that is new is quickly used by many people, and it doesn't take long before that "new" element is overused and looks dated. Fashion is a good example, as are effects in a movie, and sounds in the music business (you can instantly tell an '80s tune, even if you don't know the band, right?).

Avoid effects like WordArt, ClipArt, & out-of-the-box templates.

Charts, Data, and Graphics

Choosing or creating a great chart or graphic begins with clarity on the key point of the slide. This assumes you only have one point.

Data overload in a chart is abused as often as the bullet point. The question to ask yourself is, "If someone just barely glances, what will they understand without having to work at it?"

The best thing to do is pare down the data and the chart to the bare essentials. If it's not necessary to communicating the key point of the slide, cut it out. If it's essential to the presentation, make it the point of a different slide.

Less is more. Don't drown them in details.

First Imagine Visuals, Then Find Graphics

It might be overused, but the truth of the fact that "a picture is worth a thousand words" keeps it from becoming a total cliché.

Visuals (e.g., photos, illustrations, charts, etc.) can deliver impact that words alone on a slide won't accomplish, and they usually have one or more of the following three qualities:

Easily grasped – Does the image help the viewer quickly understand the point you are making?

Memorable – Does it improve your "stickiness?"

Tells a story – Does the image present your point with additional context that is persuasive?

To turn your key point into a visual, you need to have a clear understanding of the point you're trying to make on that slide, as well as how your audience is likely to receive it.

Start by imagining the ideal image to create that "aha!" moment for your audience. Then go find the best image you can, create the chart that communicates that point, or arrange the content of your slides to achieve it.

Great visuals are easily grasped, memorable, and tell a story. The goal is an "aha!" moment.

Image Consciousness

When using images of people, pay attention to where the attention of those people is focused. If their gaze extends, by implication, to some point of observation beyond the border of the graphic, we as humans tend to be drawn – usually unconsciously – to follow their focus. When you have a choice, face the gaze of your graphic "people" toward the middle of your slide rather than away from your content.

Face images of people into the slide.

Remain Consistent

When using graphics of various forms (e.g., photos, illustrations, clip art), give thought to the overall feel of the presentation. Do they support the tone and message of your presentation?

If your designer's eye isn't strong, one thing you can do to increase the visual cohesiveness is to stick to one type of graphic element. For instance, using all illustrations, perhaps even from the same designer, will help greatly.

Tip: Spend a little time perusing content at iStockphoto (www.istockphoto.com). Notice differences in style and texture from different designers. Choose a designer and notice how images from that designer have a similar look and feel, even when the images communicate very different ideas.

Stay consistent visually.

Rule of Thirds

To be completely fair, this book isn't a complete treatise on slide design, but one quick principle that will serve you well is the "rule of thirds."

In short, divide your slide into thirds both vertically and horizontally. Images placed at the intersections of those lines (whether imaginary or via PowerPoint ruler) are considered to be more interesting to viewers than centered images.

What I like about the rule of thirds is this: When you take any image, consider its key focal point, and position it on the slide with one of these points in mind, very often you will find perspective or tension enhanced in a way that makes it more interesting.

The question to keep asking yourself is, "What's the takeaway that I want the audience to quickly understand, and if I were in their shoes, is this helping that cause?"

Use the "rule of thirds" to improve the impact of your images.

Increasing Visual Stimulation

Imagine you are watching television and the screen is showing still images that change only every two or three minutes. How long would it take before you figured out you could look at something else, just listening in, and check back every few minutes to make sure you hadn't missed something?

There are two things we naturally do as humans. One is that we notice change. We're wired for it. The second is that we'll go to great lengths not to to miss something.

You can use both of these to your advantage when putting together your slides.

To keep your audience engaged, keep change happening visually by creating more slides, not less. You will not only appeal to that part of the brain that notices change, but you will create an environment that screams, "If you look away, you'll miss something."

This may mean throwing out something someone else taught you about PowerPoint, but they weren't teaching you to rock in a web seminar. It's easy when you commit to having but one point (or less) per slide.

Up your audience engagement factor. Keep it moving.

Test Your Font Size

One difference in the web seminar audience's "environment" versus a live room is the size of slide they'll be viewing when watching your online presentation. Obviously it's going to be smaller than when viewed on a screen from a projector in a room.

Text that is too small fails one of the tests we applied to great visuals: It's not easily grasped. To succeed, make sure your text is large enough to be easily read when the slide is small.

Here's a quick way to stress-test your text:

1. Put PowerPoint in "normal" mode.
2. Select the main slide area and resize it to 50%.
3. Imagine just glancing at that small area and ask yourself if you can quickly get what's being said.

Note: Many web conferencing solutions offer presenters the ability to push the audience to "full screen mode" so they'll see the presentation in full-size on their screens.

DON'T TRUST IT!

Those solutions also give audience members a way to close out of full-screen view or reduce their viewing area. Given that most people multitask to some degree, don't rely on that feature and the complete, rapt attention of your audience.

Test your font size by using a reduced-size view in your presentation software.

Learning from Jeffrey Gitomer, Sales Guru

Many years ago I moderated an event for Jeffrey Gitomer, author of best sellers like *The Sales Bible* and *The Little Red Book of Selling*, et al. He showed up to speak with 109 slides to present in an hour or less. He got through the presentation in about fifty minutes, meaning he was pushing a slide about every twenty-nine seconds.

The lights went on for me. He's used to presenting to an audience with a bad case of ADHD – salespeople.

He'd learned to keep the presentation moving, and not because he was presenting to a virtual audience that's one click away from something else.

Subsequently I've discovered others who do this, such as Stanford Professor Laurence Lessig. Search the web (or use http://bit.ly/mn5vy if it's still active) and you'll find a famous presentation where he goes through 235 slides in thirty minutes.

I now coach people in this direction, and my friend Ray Taylor, President of sales consultancy Choice 32, recently did an absolutely amazing presentation about mastering LinkedIn using 145 slides in a one hour web seminar – with time left for Q&A

This might seem extreme, but it puts an exclamation point behind the idea. Invest in your audience, and they'll be calling you the next presentation software guru.

Animations

Presentation software has a feature typically referred to as "animations." An animation is something that happens on the slide when you click... a new element appears, or moves, or vanishes. Many animation elements are special effects, like the object flying into place or going away with a triple spin and half twist.

The Trouble with Animations

There are four problems with animations, at least for most presenters.

One, animations change the meaning of a click. At one point in the presentation a click advances a slide, while at another it triggers an animation. Unless you know your presentation cold, it increases the chance that you'll make a mistake.

Related, point 1.5 is the question, "What happens when you want to go backwards?" You don't do it a lot, but do you know what will happen? Does it reverse an animation or does it go back a slide? In some cases you may have advanced several animations, but going back takes you back a whole slide. Bah humbug.

Two, web conferencing vendors treat animations differently. This is problematic enough for virtual presenters that I've given it separate treatment later.

Three, unless you're facile with PowerPoint, animations can take a lot of time to create. I give a big tip later (see "Create Fake Animations") that will change this for you.

Finally, many (most?) animatinos are a lot like clip art – a bit campy and gimmicky.

Avoid most animations.

OTOH...

To be fair, an animation is a tool, and like all tools, there's a time and place when it's the right choice to help you make a point. Here are some examples of when I use an animation:

1) Demonstrating a directional relationship between objects. For example, I use a slide representing a conference call. Arrows point between phones, but to better demonstrate that conversation occurs sequentially, I have the lines appear at different times.

2) Demonstrating movement from one point on a graphic to another. For example, I make a point about an evolutionary shift in behavior, and a red circle moves from one part of the graphic to another.

I do, however, practice what I preach, and I use animations quite sparingly. The question for you is whether the animation is the right tool for helping you make your point or whether you're just attempting to add eye candy.

Use an animation when it's the right tool for making your point.

Caveat Presentor

Adding to the challenges of using animations to create motion is the fact that all web conferencing solutions are not created equally.

Some allow no animations whatsoever, so that presentation you painstakingly created with a pile of them would need a significant overhaul.

Others treat animations differently, both for going forward and backward.

Yet another challenge is that if you're screen sharing there's a risk that your animations will appear choppy to the attendees. Sometimes it's because the web conferencing solution is slow, but *most* often it has to do with the attendee's own internet connection.

If you're searching for a web conferencing solution, it's worth discovering how each option treats animations before making a commitment (relative to your style and needs, of course). If you always use the same solution, it's worth noting how it works *before* you present... and if you often find yourself in different environments as I do, you've been warned.

Note that as presenters you already need to think ahead about your enviroment. When in person, factors such as brightness and resolution of the projector affect your presentation design and delivery. This is a similar exhortation with regard to the tools of the virtual presenter.

Know how the presentation solution treats animations.

Create Fake Animations

I like the *idea* of PowerPoint animations because it makes the visual change more quickly. But I hate animations for two reasons.

One, they're time-consuming to create.

Two, most web conferencing software can't deal with one uncontrollable fact: The least reliable part of your whole experience is your local internet service provider. Too often, audiences experience an animations as a series of jerky spasms across the screen. This doesn't improve anything.

What I use a lot of are faux animations. Here's what I mean:

Imagine you have a very simple slide with two images on it, and as you tell your story, you want one to appear immediately, while the other doesn't appear until you "click."

To achieve the same result simply create two slides:

1. Start with the finished slide, one that contains both objects (images) as you want them to appear.

2. Duplicate the slide.

3. Remove the second object from the first of the two slides.

As you advance through your deck, the same story unfolds.

And for most of us, we achieved this much more quickly than by using an animation.

Speed up the process of putting together your deck. Use multiple slides to create fake animations.

Smooth, Daddy-o

A transition is a critical juncture in your presentation. The goal of a great transition is to set up your next point by creating a logical connection between where you're coming from and where you're going. It's an opportunity to create anticipation for what's coming next. Ignored, transitions will cost you momentum.

Newscasters are genius with transitions that create momentum. They don't just say, "And now Colin will talk to us about the sports games on tap for tonight." You're more likely to hear something like, "So how will tonight's snow affect players in that game at Washington High School? For a closer look, here's Colin with…"

Consider the following:

"On this next slide you will see…

"So we have identified the problems caused by inadequate testing. The next step is to…"

"So we have identified the problems caused by inadequate testing. How are we going to improve our go-to-market plan with a solution?"

There are many ways to transition, and this simply scratches the surface of possibility. The first step is to be aware of how you transition from concept to concept.

Plan strong transitions – between thoughts and between presenters.

Guy Kawasaki's "10-20-30 Rule"

Let me start by saying I love Guy Kawasaki. I own several of his books, and I fancy myself a corporate evangelist – for the benefits of meeting and presenting online – much as he pioneered evangelizing the Mac.

That said, his "10/20/30" rule for presentations is oft quoted and almost always out of context.

Here's why:

The idea of "10 slides that go for no more than 20 minutes and have no font sizes smaller than 30 points" is his response to businessfolk making pitches to venture capitalists. His message is to a specific audience in a specific context.

Simply: Get to the point, and here's what I want to see as a VC.

As Mark Twain, who knew a little about writing, once said, "I didn't have time to write you a short letter, so I wrote a longer one instead."

And I harp on that point, too. It takes investing in your audience to develop a concise, clear message.

But that doesn't mean that ten slides is the only way to accomplish your goal. You can have ten slides and ramble like a drunken idiot.

Putting a presentation together isn't a formula (though there are a few notably good ones like Cliff Atkinson's *Beyond Bullet Points*), it's the telling of a story that gets your audience from Point A to Point B both aurally and visually. If there were only one formula, there would only be one way to write a book or produce a movie, too.

Section 6

Getting Yourself Ready

Getting Yourself Ready

Developing a Pre-Show Routine

Professional sports figures often approach a moment of performance with some form of routine. Whether it's a golfer preparing for a shot or a power lifter gearing up for a lift, what they have in common is some form of ritual that prepares them mentally for peak performance.

Actors, musicians, and yes, professional speakers similarly often have ways they approach stepping into "show mode." Whatever it is, they've been purposeful with planning and practice, dedicated to their own commitment to being the best they can be.

Have a routine.

Own It

Even if you're not a professional speaker, or presenting isn't your primary gig, I'd recommend determining in advance the things you need to do and writing them down.

If you're a guest speaker or presenter, your host may have a checklist of items to consider as you prepare for your presentation. Whether the list is theirs or yours, the key is to "own it," meaning you arrange it in terms of two things:

First, you find an order of execution that makes sense to you. This means determining how one task flows into the next.

Second, you work out a sense of timing.

Owning your pre-show checklist has one key benefit: peace of mind. Your jitters, energy, or the last minute cell phone call from the boss won't shake you. And as your list becomes more familiar – even automatic – you can focus your mental energy on your audience and content instead of sweating other details.

"Own" a pre-show checklist.

Print a Backup Copy

I know it's fifty slides long (mine are a lot longer). Print a copy of your presentation before you present.

There are two compelling reasons:

The first is risk management. The question isn't if, but when you'll experience an internet slowdown or something that will affect the performance of your web seminar (web seminar providers don't want to tell you this… though to be fair, it's not usually their fault). If the visual freezes or experiences serious latency, often one of your other presenters or behind-the-scenes partners can push the slide for you. And you'll have your printed deck to refer to. (We'll talk about the wisdom of presenting with a team later.)

The second is access to notes. Print the "notes" view. Now all the text you moved off your slide into the presenter notes is yours to refer to. And those extra annotations, anecdote reminders, etc., are at your fingertips.

Print a notes-view copy of your presentation.

Tips for Great Rehearsals

Do What the Pros Do

Imagine a professional of any kind who hasn't put in a lot of hours perfecting their skills – and who doesn't continue to do so – in order to excel at their craft. Can you think of one?

Even if you can, do you have that level of proficiency when it comes to presenting online?

Rehearsals don't have to be fancy, but they do need to occur. And as Jerry Weisman notes in *The Power Presenter*, you really should verbalize (meaning speak the words) out loud.

If you're really pressed for time and don't feel like you can spare the moment, focus on making sure your opening and closing flow well. That will help create momentum both to kick things off and to finish strong.

Much like developing your story and designing your slides, a rehearsal is an investment in your audience, and therefore in your own success.

Pros rehearse.

Not So Fast

As your adrenaline starts pumping, whether from fear or excited anticipation, you'll have a tendency to speed up. The challenge is that you risk breezing by a key point that you really want or need to make. I'll talk about delivery and the "pregnant pause" a bit later, but the point in this preparatory phase is to practice slowing down. Pay attention to your diction and clarity, and most importantly, bring to consciousness that which is unconscious.

Practice slowing down.

Too Much Stimulation

Adrenaline, part two. My doctor once asked me what happens when I stop drinking coffee. I said, "I don't know. I've never stopped."

Years later I find myself reading every book I can get my hands on about public speaking, and a common exhortation of many is "just say no to caffeine."

In reality, I've noticed that controlled vocal delivery is harder when I've had coffee or a soft drink, even if I long ago quit noticing the boost I get from caffeine.

You probably don't notice the effect of caffeine in your life, either, but you *can* notice that I'm adding myself to the long list of those who urge you to avoid it before speaking.

Don't compound the effect of adrenaline. Avoid caffeine and stimulants.

Reading Is Boring

A Marketing Sherpa survey once offered respondents a number of options for completing a question that began "How likely would you be to leave a webinar early if…" The top response was "if the webinar content was not as advertised."

The second? "If the presenter read directly from the slides."

May I extrapolate that this would also include whether the presenter reads a script? Unless you're Katie Couric or some other newscaster with prodigious skills in script-reading-while-sounding-natural, the audience will know.

That said, you need to nail your openers and closers. The first creates momentum and desire, and the latter sends your audience off to their next task with a sense of awe and accomplishment.

So the lesson is this: While you need to deliver (and really nail) some carefully chosen words, the audience willl be able to tell if you're reading. People tend to judge you most by the first and last things you say. Carefully choose your words... and don't read them.

Practice verbalizing your openers and closers.

I Can See It Now... The Whiteboard

The whiteboard is typically an instrument of a collaborative session. In a smaller session, we might engage in brainstorming or taking other input, capturing those thoughts, and writing them down for all to see. In larger, more structured, presentations we typically don't do that.

As natural as it might be to grab a pen when in person, the act of drawing on a virtual whiteboard is a good bit more computer tool-centric. You may have a pen with which you can draw free-form, but you'll probably also have tools for typing text, drawing rectangles and circles, etc. Your goal is to become comfortable with the tools you've got, where to grab them, and how to get an idea out of your head onto the virtual whiteboard.

If you're going to use a whiteboard, practice visualizing and drawing your thoughts in advance.

Like any other tool, the whiteboard can be useful if you think and plan ahead.

Record and Listen

Most people don't like the sound of their own voice when they hear it recorded. At least one factor in this is because it doesn't sound natural. We're used to hearing our own voice through the bones in our head, in addition to through our auditory canals.

Short of some voice training, there isn't much you can do about this. And even then, you have what you have.

What you *can* do, however, is get better at your delivery, and that's easy to do:

Record yourself, and then listen.

You will quickly hear yourself – your tempo, your pauses, your ums and ahs – in a new way.

Why is this SO important?

In a recent study I conducted of over more than six hundred professionals, "quality of the presenter's voice when delivering" was cited as the second most important factor in the success of a live, online presentation ("ease of use" of the web seminar software was rated first).

Since making a recording in a web conferencing tool is push-button simple, there's no excuse not to record and listen (my dog ate my mini-cassette recorder?).

Record yourself. Listen. Learn.

Mitigating Common Risk

Present with a Partner or Team

Presenting online is truly better with a team of two or more, and it's something I'd highly encourage. Consider some different scenarios:

One behind-the-scenes partner: Even if your presentation isn't a major production, you likely can easily recruit one person to hang out 'backstage.' This person can assist with questions and chat, give you time checks, or even just provide peace of mind that someone is available to push slides for you if there's a technical challenge.

You can define your partner's role however you like. The point is simply to get some help, in order to decrease the number of things you need to pay attention to while presenting.

A behind-the-scenes team: For larger events, consider a team. You *know* you will get FAQs like, "Can I have a copy of this presentation?" and "What was the telephone number again?" (even when you've addressed it four times already!). One rule of thumb we used in the event production biz is having one helper for every fifty people you expect in the audience.

One especially common scenario is the presentation where you don't want to answer direct product/feature or pricing questions. Recruiting a few assistants from your sales team is a great tactic. Just be sure to agree ahead of time on the nature of the answers, so that everyone will be on the same page. Examples may include whether to answer questions directly, possibly providing the sales team's 800 number, or privately sending those prospects the contact name/number of the account manager.

Work with a team for best results.

Engage a Moderator

Even with a behind-the-scenes team, adding a moderator adds value. This 'color commentator' will amplify your connection with the audience, from delivering your bio with credibility, to teeing up questions and comments, to making the closing remarks.

A great moderator will join the virtual stage with you and make you look like a rock star. Use a kick-butt moderator.

The Set Up

The best way to get started on the right note is a great introduction (provided by that kick-butt moderator you engaged). Having a good bio delivered by a moderator or emcee will not only set up your credibility with authority, it'll set the event in motion and give you a running start.

Don't forget a good bio.

Get It Done. Now.

In the virtual world, it's common for an event coordinator
to ask for your slides to be delivered early, often twenty-
four to forty-eight hours in advance. Their job is to
make sure your slides are ready to go relative to the
presentation technology. Treat this like the wisdom you've
heard about showing up to an in-person venue early,
checking out the room, and making sure your goods look
great on the projector.

Here are a couple things I've experienced that you might
run into:

- I've found at the last minute that a company's email
servers had an imposed size limit. Minutes before the
event I get a message saying, "Sorry, your email was
rejected because it's too big."

- I've had a deck become mysteriously corrupt. Mere
moments before an event isn't the time to figure out
which of the last saved versions wasn't corrupt, make
some edits, and try to make it work.

- I've had a deck that for some mysterious reason
wouldn't upload into the web conferencing software,
despite the fact that it had worked fine during
rehearsal.

Getting your deck to the coordinator doesn't mean you
can't make last minute changes (though if you're trying to
make too many changes, you should probably re-examine
your approach). I almost *always* make a couple final
tweaks, but they're typically so minor (e.g., a typo or

slight change of phrase) that if needed I can easily describe the change to someone else who can take care of it.

Get your slides done and to the moderator and event producer early.

Practice Properly

Different computers come with different configurations, from operating system to software – even within the same company. It's one of life's mysteries, so you have to learn to live with it. My goal is to give you every way possible to minimize the chances of something going wrong on the big day.

To minimize those chances, practice your presentation using the same computer you'll be working from on the big day.

Practice from the computer you're going to present from.

Section 7

Delivering Like a Rockstar

Delivering Like a Rockstar

Backstage

Some Reminders...

It's common to be nervous. You're almost not normal if you don't get nervous. The goal shouldn't necessarily to avoid being so, but to have the presence of mind to know how it's likely to affect you and what to do about it.

The two most common things that happen when your adrenaline is flowing are that your tempo speeds up and your breathing gets shallow. You might not avoid these, but you can respond to them.

First, remember to avoid caffeine. It increases your blood pressure, and increases the likelihood that you'll speed up.

Second, breathe. Deeply. Slowly. And from your gut (the diaphragm). Get the breath down below your chest. Feel your abdomen slowly expand and gently contract. The oxygen will do good things for you.

Third, slow down. You can't speak as quickly as you can think, and you can't speak as quickly as others think (or read, for that matter). But if you're going too fast, you'll barrel past great opportunities to pause for effect or provide other inflection that helps deliver your point with emphasis.

Slow down. Breathe. And breathe again.

Close It Up

Web conferencing tools are software. This means they're not perfect (no software is), and this means they potentially conflict with other software. At the very least, your computer has a finite amount of power available, and you want every potential ounce of computing resource focused on the success of your presentation.

Close all applications that aren't part of the presentation.

Clear the Decks

Following the previous point, here's something that I do every single time I present: Reboot. Just because you closed all other applications doesn't mean that your computing power is now fully focused on the task at hand. It's like insurance – you're not counting on having an accident, but you're prepared in case. Be prepared.

Reboot.

Prevent Popups

Depending on your computer's configuration, there may be some things that start up (such as instant messaging) when you boot your machine. If you're sharing from your desktop during a presentation, you do not want to get a message or calendar notification... especially when you thought everything else was turned off.

Make sure email, IM, and any other popups are disabled.

Cotton Mouth

Even pros get a rush of energy or nerves when presenting. And a common byproduct of stress is a dry mouth. If you forget a glass of water and this happens to you, one experience of presenting when it feels like you have a mouth full of cotton balls should help you remember this proposition the next time. Or you could spare yourself the pain and...

...have a glass of water.

Good Vibrations

Part of your backstage routine should be turning off your cell phone, sort of.

Many folks will tell you to turn off your cell phone in order to prevent an interruption, but I've got an alternative for you.

Most of the time when you present, the presentation team will be on an operator-assisted conference call. One thing most operators won't ask, but are capable of doing, is calling you and patching you back into the conference call if your connection drops. Give the operator your cell phone number, put your phone on vibrate, and know that you're covered in the event that your primary line drops the call.

How often does this happen? Not very. The telephone system is one of the most reliable technologies available. For me I think it's happened twice in ten years, but one of them was in early 2009 in front of several hundred attendees. It's not fun, but it's even less fun if you're not prepared.

Put your mobile phone on vibrate, and give the operator the phone number.

Plan Your Spontaneity

Assuming you want to sound natural and comfortable, here's a technique for those moments of brain-freeze: Plan to be spontaneous.

As you move through your content, whether before rehearsal or as you verbalize your presentation, you will probably think of places that human interaction would be natural (either asking the audience a question or the audience asking one of you).

Use your presentation notes to jot those places down.

Don't leave spontaneity to chance – plan to be spontaneous.

If Necessary, Plant

But what if I don't have a question from the audience?
Plant one. Or make one up on the fly ("Hey, George has a
pertinent question. He asks...").

On occasion someone asks if I think this is being fake. I
don't think so, and this is why:

If you have any depth at all in the subject you're
presenting on (and you likely do... that's why you're
presenting), you are intimately familiar with the most
frequently asked questions. You probably also have some
great answers to the most common objections. Bringing
one of these up yourself is simply addressing the question
head-on.

When you've demonstrated that you'll answer questions
this way, more will come in. No one in the audience has
to feel like they're the first or are all alone, and everyone
benefits.

Plan to use "ad hoc" questions.

Prepare Your Moderator

Parallel to planning your spontaneity, don't leave your
planted questions to chance, either.

Before your presentation, ask yourself (and write down the
answers) to two questions:

"What questions would I love to get from the audience?"

"What questions do I hope to avoid?"

Then make sure to share what you've identified with the moderator of the event. A good moderator will use them as a guide when s/he chooses which questions from the audience to ask you. Or s/he will ask those exact questions (the good ones, anyway) to improve interactivity if the audience had too much turkey for lunch.

Prep the moderator with a few planted questions.

A Moderator's Confession

I was moderating an event for a client with an audience that was primarily in India. Registration was light, but they wanted to go through with the presentation anyway so they could make a recording to post on their website.

As is my custom, I told the presenter that my role and goal as a moderator was to make them look like a rock star, I felt out their comfort level with taking questions during the presentation, and I asked them what questions they'd love to be asked and what kind they'd like to avoid.

During the poorly-attended presentation the audience was silent, but that didn't mean we didn't have an interactive presentation.

"Hey Pete, Anoop asks...," "Pradeep asks a relevant question, Pete," and "Here's one from Bhaskar..." were the order of the day.

At the end of the presentation the operator put the presentation team back into a sub-conference call so we could speak amongst ourselves. The event's sponsor asked about the Q&A, commenting that she hadn't seen any Q&A coming in and hadn't noticed any Anoop in the audience. My answer: I've been in the software business a long time, and I know many Indian people as a result. I simply started calling out the first names of past co-workers, saying they had questions (those the presenter had given me in advance).

Voila! Interactive presentation!

On Stage

May I Have Your Attention? Please?

Quick poll: Do you have a cell phone, iPhone, Blackberry, or laptop? Have you ever used it during a meeting?

The reality is that today's audience is multi-tasking during your presentation, perhaps even twittering about it in real time. Even in an in-person environment, where there's more social pressure to look engaged, you can count on not having your audience's undivided attention.

Assume they're multi-tasking.

Details, Details

One handy way to share audio conferencing details with the audience is to use the chat function. You can do this prior to the beginning of the presentation so it's the very first entry in everyone's chat log. This gives them one more place to find the phone number, and it beats someone being late because they can't find the right email.

Another thing you can do is copy/paste a link into chat, perhaps as an on-the-fly way of sharing with the audience.

Get creative. Chat doesn't have to just be questions.

Show, Don't Tell

Unfortunately your audience's expectations for webinars is similar to the way they anticipate the average meeting. Meetings generally suck. This means that they're going to assume that you're going to be nothing more compelling than an ambient voice in the room from a speaker phone – unless you demonstrate otherwise.

Even if you plan to engage people throughout the presentation, you'll lose them to a speaker phone and email if you don't demonstrate early your intention to be different.

It's not enough to have a welcome script in which the moderator states, "We'll have an interactive session," and "We'll answer your questions." They've heard that before.

Show, don't tell the audience VERY early how interactivity is going to occur.

Questions, Anyone?

A typical audience – again accustomed to presentation boredom – will not ask a lot of questions… *until* they see that you're going to do something about it. Answer a question early, and you'll usually see the quantity of questions asked leap up.

Answer an audience question early.

Call for a Vote

A poll is a great way to demonstrate interactivity.

When you open a poll it will take a little time for folks to vote. If we assume they're multi-tasking, you'll want to get their attention. A poll provides an opportunity to interrupt them. You've got an opportunity to increase the percentage of the audience that votes in your poll:

Verbally cue the audience to participate in polls.

Know When to Say "When"

Someone's not paying attention, that's guaranteed. Someone else got a call on their mobile phone, and another got up to pay a visit to the water closet (U.S. translation: "the restroom").

Most web conference solutions allow you to see the total audience population, as well as the quantity that has voted in the poll (though these data points don't usually appear next to each other visually).

If you wait for complete participation you'll likely be waiting too long... and testing the patience of those who are with keeping up with you.

Don't expect 100% participation in polls.

FAQ: What percentage of the audience should I let vote before closing and sharing?

A: This is more an art than a science, and I usually expect something in the mid- or upper-80% range. I'd use this analogy as a guide: When you pop popcorn, if you wait for every kernel to be popped, you'll burn some of it. Instead, you wait until the popping slows down, using intuition to determine when to stop. You might have instructions that say "when popping slows to about one pop per second," or some such thing, but it's still just a guide that you have to adjust based on your own cooking tools. Same here.

Closed Polling

If someone thinks they have a wrong answer, especially if they think you can identify by person how they voted, there's a chance they'll change their answer to fit in with the group or a majority vote.

Many web conferencing solutions have a couple features that help you improve the accuracy of your poll result:

One, you can close the poll, freezing the results and preventing further votes or changes.

Two, you can keep the results from the audience's view.

Keep poll results hidden until an adequate percentage of the audience has voted.

Grab a Pen

Another piece of advice about creating impact when delivering a virtual presentation: Tell 'em to grab a pen.

When you're coming up on one of your key points in a virtual presentation, remember a common 1080 Group exhortation: Assume they're multitasking.

Q: So how do you get their attention?

A: Get literal. Pause, say "Are you ready? Grab a pen."

One, you create some anticipation. They don't know what's going to come next. In a world raised on radio ads spouting 800 numbers at you when you can't write anything down, I find this tactic works.

Two, you're communicating that 'this is important.' And, well, it is. Or it better be.

Tell 'em to grab a pen.

Make Friends with Annotation Tools

The first rule of avoiding multi-tasking is "don't suck." The second is a corollary: Provide visual cues for the audience, to show them what they should be looking at… which means you have to command and focus attention.

Even before you've become adept at developing slides that keep things moving visually, you can use a pointer or annotation tool of some sort to visually draw attention to the portion of the slide you're speaking to. In a screen share the audience will see your mouse pointer. Most web conferencing solutions provide some form of annotation tools, such as pointers, arrows, or highlighters.

Use annotation tools to focus attention.

The 'Hand Up' Tool Is Good, Too

Unless you're delivering a keynote, you'll likely be delivering content in a way that means that during your presentation, you'll think of questions worthy of asking the audience. It happens naturally when we're in a group of people, but it can be just as natural when we're virtual.

Remember to use your Hand Up tool to keep an eye on when your audience might need some extra attention.

Use a 'hand up' tool for ad hoc answers.

A Couple Useful Hand Up Tips

One, even if it's included in the welcome script, when you're opening the floor for questions, remind the audience how to participate.

Two, if you can, give them specific verbal directions such as, "In the upper-right hand part of your attendee console, if you open the gray window you will see…"

Finally, if you're not going to use Hand Up and you have the option turn it off, do so. Otherwise, attendees will put their hand up and get frustrated when you don't respond, even if you've demonstrated you're not using it or are using other tools for communicating. I wouldn't say 'assume your audience is full of idiots,' but I'd assume there's one in the crowd.

Repeat how you're going to interact.

Rhythm and Pacing and Flow (oh my)

Another easy way to add impact to your presentation is to employ a technique that storytellers, comedians, and news anchors have been using for eons: the pregnant pause. Paul Harvey was my favorite demigod at this, but you don't have to have been broadcasting for sixty years to add it to your bag of tricks.

The pregnant pause is simply a pause or hesitation that heightens the tension or creates anticipation... ...and then releases to deliver optimum impact to what is said right after the pause. The reason this is so powerful is simple. Our sensory systems tend to most readily pick up changes, differences, or disruption. Someone in your audience who is only half-listening is most likely to be drawn back when something interrupts their zoning out. Da da da da DA da DA... ...da DA!

To start, become consciously aware of the tempo, or pace, of your delivery. Speak too quickly and you'll sound frenetic or nervous; too slowly and you'll put 'em to sleep. Either way, having an awareness of how you sound to someone else is a step toward being a pro. Remember "record and listen?"

To use a musical analogy, just like a drummer sets the pace (tempo) of a tune, they also set forth emphases, or rhythms, that become recognizable... that's how you recognize the beat as rock, hip hop, or bossa nova.

This 'rhythm' element isn't something you're going to apply to a whole business presentation. But there may be elements – such as the three key points that you repeat –

that you emphasize in a rhythmic way. Da da da da DA da DA da DA! I don't suggest manufacturing something, but make it a point to consciously avoid the monotone and lean toward the drama already inherent in how the words flow.

Command attention. Master the pregnant pause.

Repeat Yourself

There are multiple ways to deliver a point with emphasis, and since web/audio conferencing events (mostly) eliminate the value of you waving your arms around wildly, it's helpful to give the audience a visual clue that you're making an important point.

One of my favorite speakers, whose personal mission is teaching, is a master at repeating his key phrases. Not only does he repeat the soundbite when he makes the point, he brilliantly transitions to the next point by repeating his first.

The lesson learned, if we feebly attempt to turn it into a formula, looks like this:

1. Literally repeat the phrase. If appropriate, change up where you place an accent.

"Sometimes the the enemy of the *best* is the good."

"Sometimes the *enemy* of the best is the *good*."

2. Use a repeat of the phrase both to summarize and close one point, but also to set up or transition to the next point:

"…sometimes the enemy of the best is the good. And what does this demand of us? We can't say *NO* to good things until we get clear on the one thing. We can't say no to good things… until we get clear on *the one thing*."

Repeat for emphasis and transition.

When the Stuff Hits the Fan

Planning for the Unplannable – What Happens When It Goes Wrong

Fact #1 when using technology is that sometimes it fails. Fact #2 is refer to fact #1.

The good news is that the POTS – the plain old telephone system – has been around for decades and is as close to bullet proof as technology comes. Computers aren't.

Short of a complete failure, it's not uncommon for many technologies to experience latency, meaning a delay of some sort. This is sometimes experienced as a delay between when you click "next slide" and when it advances. If you're doing a screen share, your audience may experience a little choppiness.

There are two realities to be aware of here.

One, reliability is one thing that separates the major solution providers from the smaller players. The delta between the two is decreasing, but the fact remains that reliability is a sizable investment that only well-funded companies can take to an advanced level.

Two, the worst part of any web conferencing system is a two-part quandary over which nobody has control. The first is your personal computer. The second is your local internet connection.

The question when presenting online is not *if* something will go wrong, but *when*. If you approach it as such, 98% of the time you'll never have to worry. The other 2% of the time, remember the following maxim:

Professionalism isn't what happens when everything goes right. Professionalism is what happens when everything goes wrong.

What Not to Do

Now that you've been warned, you can be prepared to weather what comes along. There is no magic bullet or "one size fits all" response, but remember this: If you don't draw attention to a mistake or problem, most people won't notice.

To be sure, the presentation team will be sweating, a moment of silence will seem like an hour, and the voice in your head will want to start apologizing or explaining. But the audience will most likely never notice. I promise.

Don't make it obvious.

Another thing you'll want to do is to blame.

Don't blame.

Stories from the Front

As Vice President of Client Services for a web seminar production company, one of the first things I'd teach new event producers was what to expect from a client if an event were to go sideways.

The client's first reaction is to save face in front of *their* clients and supervisor(s). When a problem arose, our response needed to be silence and empathy in the moment, offering a promise for a full investigation. Once a little time had passed, usually a day, we'd deliver a full report of what occurred – no blame, just facts. (And of course if we were at fault in any way we'd provide an offer to make good.)

Our report was delivered in a written form that was easily shared, and written from a point of view that meant the document could be forwarded to supervisors or other interested parties, thus saving the client the need to be able to remember and explain things themselves.

Inevitably, once the emotions of the moment had passed, all but the most obstinate clients could see things more clearly, accept the unchangeable facts, and prepare how to move forward.

What we should take away from this is a point of self-awareness. I've been on the other side of the presentation, and I've received email saying "that was the worst presentation ever," when the problem had nothing to do with me as the presenter or with the content. To be sure, it stings. But nobody is served by pointing fingers, and while your own emotions will still roil, your next step to success is the same as any other time – have an attitude that little setbacks aren't going to stop you from reaching your goals.

When the Inevitable Occurs

If something goes sideways, take a breath. It seems like a lot longer for you than anyone else. If the slide still doesn't move, that's why you've got that printed copy of your presentation.

Gently say "next slide please."

Better Still...

As you gain experience, you'll become a little less flustered by latency or other hiccups, and will find you can even hide the fact that anything is amiss. An attentive team member will know exactly where you are, and you can simply give verbal nods that they'll respond to. That's why you have them there.

Better yet, say "on this next slide you will see…"

Moderator, Anyone?

Team member? Recall I've recommended presenting with someone else – for numerous reasons. Often the behind-the-scenes producers aren't themselves presentation personalities. A rocking moderator will have the presence of mind and experience to cover you, especially if the delay is extended for any reason. They'll feed you questions for an ad hoc Q&A or dialogue, they'll have an unflustered sense of when to go ahead and continue with an audio presentation, they'll deflect issues from you and give the audience instructions about what to do next…

…which is why I say, "Use a kick-butt moderator!"

Make It Right

If you're charging a fee to participants, make sure you've got a policy in place spelling out what you're going to do in the event of failure, their absence, their desire to substitute another attendee, and all the things you'd otherwise have in a policy for. In this, web conferencing is no different than any other product or service you'd offer.

If the event is free, the participants have still paid you with their time. It's still wise to figure out how you're going to serve them. You reached out to them for a reason, and they responded for a reason. Offer another session or offer a personal demo or presentation – and do so with the same attitude that says "professionalism isn't what happens when something goes right, it's what happens when something goes wrong."

Offer a handout, personal demo, or appropriate option to make good.

Keep an Eye on Q&A

If something goes wrong, your audience will let you know… but you have to be looking at the Q&A manager to see it. If you learn to keep an eye on no other tool, this is the one to know. Use it to keep track of dialogue of all kinds, including catching wind of trouble.

If there *is* trouble, you'll need to make a quick value judgment. One person out of seventy saying "I'm not hearing anything" may not be worth stopping the show; but five people saying the same thing indicates that it's not an isolated issue.

Related side note: When I was at PlaceWare/Microsoft we tracked support calls related to web seminars. Seventy percent of issues were individual, and most of those were user error (e.g., lost passwords, speaker volume turned down or off, trying to listen through the computer speakers when the event was only using telephone conference for audio, etc.). The takeaway:

Having an audience member experience a problem is never desirable, but it's no different than if they got stuck behind an accident on the way to your in-person event. You'll have to make a value judgment about what to do, but I'd suggest you serve well the other folks who there and ready to roll instead of worrying about the one.

Watch text-based Q&A for indicators of trouble.

At the End of the Presentation

Stay On the Line

If you're on an operator-assisted conference call, at the end of the presentation the operator can put you and the rest of the presentation team back into a private sub-conference call. Do it.

If nothing else, this is a great opportunity to indulge in a little congratulatory backstage backslapping. But I'd also recommend using the time for some constructive criticism. The event will never be more fresh in your minds, and it's a great opportunity to review something that didn't go well... for next time.

Use post-conference time for event review.

A Final Word...

The Big Request

I confess I like Tony Robbins.

Once about fifteen years ago a company that I worked sent me and some co-workers to one of his shows at the local megastadium. And for all the hollering, turn-and-rub-your-neighbor's-shoulders camaraderie, and motivational bling of the day, do you what I remember?

He asked a rhetorical question: "How many ideas does it take to change your life?"

Over ten years of presenting virtually, I've made every mistake possible. I made a lot of bad presentations before I made my first good one, and I'm still improving.

And you will too. One day at a time, one idea at a time, you can change your life and your world.

Here's THE BIG REQUEST:

If you've heard me present, you know I don't talk AT an audience, I talk WITH them. It's a core value of mine, and I've now been practicing long enough to do it pretty okay.

I don't want to write at an audience, either.

If you got something out of this book, would you kindly share it with me? What struck you? What one idea might take your online presentations to the next level?

And if you didn't, would you let me know what you were expecting? What would have totally rocked your world that you didn't find here?

We're better together than apart. Join me?

Peace,

Roger Courville
1080 Group, LLC
roger@1080group.com
503.329.1662

Acknowledgements

Scott, who first believed in me enough to recruit me out of sales into product marketing. Then to later start two companies with me as a partner. And above all, a beloved friend.

Skip (still hanging in there at Microsoft): the first guy to train me about what web conferencing even was.

Bruce (now COO of Eventbuilder.com) whom I met when sitting in the lobby at EnvoyGlobal when I arrived for my first day: "Can I help you?" he asked. "I think I work here," I answered. "Welcome," he says. "I own the place."

JC: still biting my lip.

Robb: still amazed that you could have 17 instant messaging windows open at a time...and working them all effectively.

Ed, Patrick, Lindsay, and the earliest crew at Corvent: without a doubt, I learned more with you and from you in a short period of time than ever before.

The 1080 Group team, past and present: I'm honored and humbled by your pure talent.

My wife, without whose editing and publishing talents I'd be hosed.

Friends from PlaceWare, still believing in a dream that we can do more than push slides. We can change lives for the better. I WILL make it to the next reunion.

And beyond number, friends and fans at Citrix Online, Webex, Adobe, Microsoft, Intercall, Elluminate, HP, Brainshark, DimDim, Accuconference, Stream57, Virtual Marketing, The Presentation Company, GAN Conferencing, The Chariot Group, Yugma...

About the Author

Roger Courville is a ten-year veteran of web seminars and presentations – from startup to Microsoft to co-founding two companies with partner and industry veteran Scott Driscoll.

1080 Group is a training and consulting firm providing companies with knowledge and skills to better communicate and compete with virtual presentations by teaching trainers, marketers, and salespeople how to design, promote, and deliver innovative web seminars and presentations. Our team has a collective experience that includes hundreds of clients, thousands of web seminars, and more than a million web seminar attendees.

Additional 1080 Group Resources:

www.theVirtualPresenter.com - Roger's blog and book (*The Virtual Presenter's Handbook*)

www.webseminartips.com - one web seminar production tip, twice monthly

www.twitter.com/1080Group - Roger on Twitter

www.webseminartoolkit.com - tools, templates, and wisdom for web seminar producers